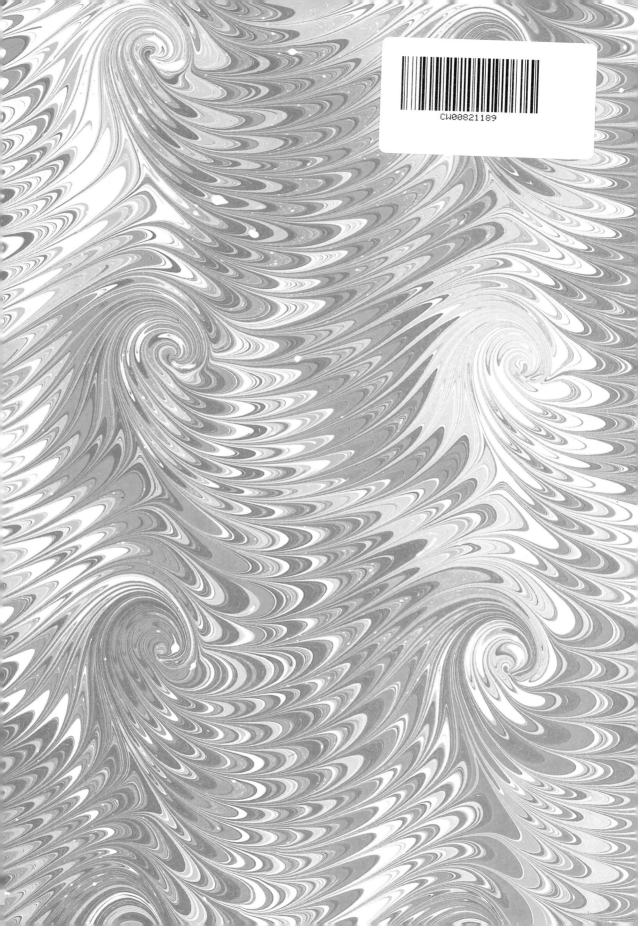

German FLAK
in WWII
1939-1945

Werner Müller

Schiffer Military/Aviation History
Atglen, PA

Sources

Koch, Horst-Adalbert, "Flak", 2nd ed., Friedberg, Podzun-Pallas-Verlag, 1965.
Nicolaisen, Hans-Dietrich, "Gruppenfeuer und Salventakt", Vol. I-II, Büsum, Selbstverlag, 1993.
Renz, Otto Wilhelm von, "Deutsche Flugabwehr im 20. Jahrhundert", Frankfurt, Mittler Verlag, 1960.
Senger-Etterlin, "Die deutschen Geschütze 1939-1945", 3rd ed., Lehmann Verlag, 1973.

Information for friends and patrons of the Museum für historische Wehrtechnik, Rötelbach, plus Luftwaffen-Dienstvorschriften (L.Dv., L.Dv.T., and L.(Luft)T.

Photo Credits

Federal Archives, Koblenz (BA) 167
From their private collections, valuable pictures were made available by: Günter Deutschmann, Guben; Wolfgang Fleischer, Freital-Wurgwitz; Michael Foedrowicz, Hannover; Reinhard Frank, Gilching; Dr. Hans Gugg, Berchtesgaden; Walter Hassenpflug, Ludwigsau-Friedlos; Henry Hoppe, Berlin; Klaus Keller-Uhl, Konstanz; Dr. Wilfried Kiefer, Reutlingen; Wolfgang Kopperschmidt, Hamburg; Norbert Krüger, Essen; Otto Menzel, Berlin; Klemens Mucha, Kaufbeuren; Werner Müller, Bad Hersfeld; Dr. Hans-Dietrich Nicolaisen, Büsum; Alfred Otte, Hannover; Heinz Riediger, Alnstadt; Prof. Dr. Wolfgang Sawodny, Elchingen; Michael Schmeelke, Friedrichshafen; Dr. Volker Seufert, Heidelberg; Volker Suhany, Wetzlar; Werner Sünkel, Leimburg; Fritz Trenkle, Freising.

The cover picture shows the 88 mm Flak in a position near Sprendlingen. The picture was taken on June 21, 1940, as part of a test series of color slides by the Leitz and Agfa firms.

Translated from the German by Ed Force

Copyright © 1998 by Schiffer Publishing, Ltd.
Library of Congress Catalog Number: 97-80167

Printed in China.
ISBN: 0-7643-0399-6

This book was originally published under the title, *FLAK im Einsatz 1939-1945* by Podzun-Pallas.

We are interested in hearing from authors with book ideas on related topics.

Published by Schiffer Publishing Ltd.
4880 Lower Valley Road
Atglen, PA 19310
Phone: (610) 593-1777
FAX: (610) 593-2002
E-mail: Schifferbk@aol.com
Please write for a free catalog.
This book may be purchased from the publisher.
Please include $3.95 postage.
Try your bookstore first.

Werner Müller

German
FLAK
in World War II
1939-1945

CONTENTS

Foreword

This book deliberately avoids a thorough description of the Flak weapons and equipment, since this has already been presented in the author's previous books.

Many of the pictures shown here were taken by amateurs. Thus they do not always live up to present-day standards of quality. We believe, though, that we should publish them nevertheless, on account of their originality and directness in portraying events.

Hearty thanks to all those who have made pictures available for this book.

The book at hand shows in pictures, for the most part not previously published, the Flak guns in their infinite uses.

In the short texts, these actions can by no means be described individually. If contradictions should appear among the cited statistics, this is because the available material is incomplete, and even original dates sometimes do not match. Substantiated facts are therefore welcome.

This 88 mm Flak 18 belonged to a battery that was located at Sprendlingen, near Frankfurt, in 1940.

German Flak in the Spanish Civil War 1936-1939

In 1936, during the years when the German Flak artillery was being built up, a civil war began in Spain between the right-wing nationalist movement under the leadership of General Franco and a communistic popular-front government. After Franco had asked the German and Italian governments for help in the form of military support. A volunteer group, the "Condor Legion", was formed in Germany, consisting of men from the Wehrmacht divisions of Army, Navy and Luftwaffe. This action offered an opportunity to test new weapons—like the Flak guns—in combat. In the course of this civil war, five 88 mm Flak batteries and two 20 mm Flak batteries saw action; one of them was partly armed with 37 mm Flak guns. The Flak of the "Condor Legion" was at first used exclusively for anti-aircraft defense. But, as the Spanish nationality units were lacking in artillery, the Flak guns had to be used more and more in the front lines to support the infantry in ground combat. The fast-firing 88 mm and 20 mm guns with their armor-piercing and time-fuse shells were very successful when used against tanks, bunkers and specific targets of all kinds. For such ground action, the usual arrangement of four 88 mm guns in a square, as set up for anti-aircraft action, was done away with; in its place, a diamond-shaped arrangement was chosen, so as to have three guns near the front for ground combat use. The fourth gun, along with the command device, was ready to fire on air targets. On the basis of this new awareness that Flak guns could also be used successfully against ground targets, a comparison firing of all kinds of artillery at concrete bunkers and other field fortifications took place in 1938 at the artillery firing range in Jüterbog, in the presence of Hitler and Göring. The best results were scored by the 88 mm Flak gun. This successful demonstration of these guns led later, in World War II, to the frequent use of more Flak weapons against ground targets than for anti-aircraft defense, which often resulted in heavy losses.

During the Spanish Civil War of 1936-39, German volunteers of the "Condor Legion" fought on the right-wing nationalist side under the command of General Franco. Here a 20 mm Flak 30 of this unit is seen in action near Toledo in 1939. (BA)

Tensely, the gun leader and crew of this 20 mm Flak of the "Condor Legion" observe the enemy's movements near Toledo in 1939. (BA)

After firing on a ground target, the 20 mm Flak 30 had to be lifted back onto the sandbags under it. (BA)

German volunteers of the "Condor Legion", along with Spanish soldiers from Franco's troops, move a 20 mm Flak gun into position in a well-constructed trench system near Toledo at the end of March 1939. (BA)

A German 20 mm Flak gun of the "Condor Legion" fires at ground targets of the Communistic People's Front. (BA)

The crew of a German 88 mm Flak gun of the "Condor Legion" cleans their gun with a barrel cleaner at a Spanish airfield after combat activity. In the foreground lies a row of bombs, ready for action. In the left background is the Special Trailer 53 for the battery's Command Assistance Device 35. (BA)

The crew of this 88 mm Flak of the "Condor Legion" had elevated the barrel to 85 degrees for cleaning. Apparently they do not expect an enemy bomb attack, for there is no splinter protection around the gun. (BA)

Flak Guns in World War II

In the summer and autumn of 1939, there were established in the Luftwaffe's Flak artillery, in the course of concealed mobilization: 657 heavy (s) batteries with about 2,600 88 mm, 105 mm and Czech Skoda guns; 560 light and medium batteries with some 6,700 20 and 37 mm guns, plus about 1,300 anti-aircraft searchlights (Sw); 188 Flak-Sw batteries with about 1,700 150 cm searchlights.

In the Army, there were only eight Flak battalions when the war began, and they were slowly being upgraded from Fla-MG to 20 mm Flak 38 guns. In the Navy there were, in addition to the AA guns carried on warships, twelve heavy and one light/medium Flak companies, primarily intended for the protection of naval bases, harbors, naval fortification areas and heavy naval artillery units. With these numbers of available guns, only focal-point areas, such as around Berlin, Hamburg and a few industrial areas in the west, could be protected so that the three-to-five fold overlapping of firepower over the protected object was attained. The attacker was supposed to be struck before reaching the bomb-dropping zone, or at least prevented from making a pinpoint attack. Smaller objects such as bridges, air stations and airfields were often protected by a mixed unit with three heavy (s) and two light/medium batteries, while multiples of these were required to protect larger cities. This formation of focal points was carried on until the war ended, even when the number of available guns of all calibers had increased considerably. This meant, though, that many cities and individual objects had to go without anti-aircraft protection, much as they needed it. The most tragic example of this was probably Dresden. Here, at the time of the destructive attacks of February 13-14, 1945, there were a few captured Russian 85 mm guns that had been modified to take the German 88 mm caliber. These guns were manned for the most part by Luftwaffe helpers, these being schoolboys drafted into the Luftwaffe from Dresden schools; they were powerless against the attacking streams of bombers. Thus, a faulty relationship, particularly after America's entry into the war, developed between available Flak guns and the need for protection.

The strength statistics for Flak guns in the war years were:

1939	657 heavy,	560 light batteries
1940	791 heavy,	686 light batteries
1941	967 heavy,	752 light batteries
1942	1,148 heavy,	892 light batteries
1943	2,132 heavy,	1,460 light batteries
1944	2,655 heavy,	1,612 light batteries

In 1945, the numbers decreased very strongly through heavy losses. Thus, in April there were 500 overworked batteries on the Oder front alone. Lack of mobility, insufficient ammunition supplies, and crews—some of which had had only brief training—led to these high losses despite their brave service. In addition, all fixed guns had to be destroyed when the troops retreated.

Standing in a row here are a 37 mm Flak 18, a 150 cm Flak Searchlight 34, two 88 mm Flak 18 and another 37 mm Flak gun.

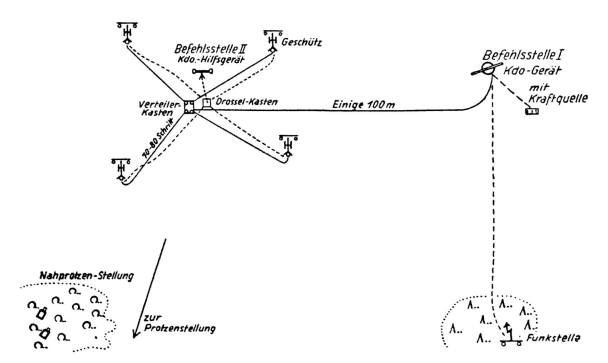

Befehlsstelle II
Kdo.-Hilfsgerät

Geschütz

Befehlsstelle I
Kdo-Gerät
mit
Kraftquelle

Verteiler-Kasten

Drossel-Kasten

Einige 100 m

70-80 Schritt

Nahprotzen-Stellung

zur
Protzenstellung

Funkstelle

This sketch map shows an 88 mm Flak battery in firing position.

A heavy Flak battery in firing position was made up, when the war began, of:

Command Post I with Command Device 36 (Crew I: 13), later Command Device 40 (Crew I: 5), the battery chief, the targeting officer, and the crew of Targeting Troop I. The device was some 100 meters away from the center of the battery in order to allow its crew to work undisturbed. The position difference was calculated by the command device. Telephone connections were made via 108-strand cables to a distributor box and from there to each gun. In addition, the shot values were transmitted through the cable, either via a light system or later by a sequence indicator.

Command Post II with the Auxiliary Command Device 35 (Kdo.Hi.Ger. 35) and Targeting Troop II. The B II was in the center of the firing position and transmitted fire control if B I was put out of action. Transmission of shot values was done only by telephone to the guns. At B II were the Battery Officer, the leader of the in telligence unit, the ammunition NCO and the gas-protection NCO.

Firing position with four 88 mm or 105 mm guns. These were located in a quadrilateral, each some 70 to 80 paces from the B II, according to the terrain.

Light Flak troop, with two (later also three) 20 mm Flak guns set up so that they could fight off a low-flying attack on the battery.

Radio position with a 100-watt transmitter, likewise located to the side of the firing position and in telephone connection with B I.

Vehicle location in a place protected from enemy air and ground sight, where the tractors, special trailers and other vehicles of the battery were placed. Depending on the terrain, they were at an appropriate distance from the firing position.

Setting up the guns varied according to their combat tasks. The four guns were set up near the front so that at least three of them could fight the attacking enemy in direct fire on ground targets without endangering one of their own guns.

Very soon, a position with an electric range finder (FuMG) was set up near B1; its values were transmitted either vocally via the command device or electrically by cable to the indicator system. In addition, in the German war zone a bunker for the "Malsi" Flak revaluing device was built near the equipment stand of B1. With the help of this simple device, shot values of a neighboring battery could be received and converted to shot values for the battery, and transmitted to it vocally, in case their own FuMG was knocked out and they had no sight of the target. With it, a difference in position of up to eight kilometers could be either included or eliminated. In order to increase the firepower of the 88 mm batteries, the formation of double or triple batteries, with eight and twelve guns, took place during the war, and eventually giant batteries of up to 24 guns were formed. In them there were three command devices and two or three FuMGs.

The following outline shows the variety of the Flak weapons used during the war. They were classified according to an order of the ObdL-Lw Fü Stab-Ia of February 23, 1943, as follows:

Light Flak: up to 36 mm
Medium Flak: 37 to 59 mm
Heavy Flak: 60 to 159 mm
Heaviest Flak: 160 mm and up

Flak-MG
MG 81 (7.9 mm) on Twin Mount 815
MG 150/15 (15 mm) on triple mount, also on Sd.Kfz. 251/21
MG 150/20 (20 mm) on triple mount (20 mm), also on Sd.Kfz. 251/21

Toward the end of the war, the guns listed above came from the realm of on-board aircraft weapons to be used as anti-aircraft machine guns in the German war zone, at airfields and on shore patrol boats. To protect railroad transport, they were carried instead of the 20 mm or 37 mm Flak guns. The weapons were mounted on socket mounts and stood free or were set in light Flak mounts like the 30 mm on-board guns.

Light Flak
20 mm MG C/30
20 mm Flak 30, also mounted on Sd.Kfz. 10 and, for ground combat, on ground mount
20 mm Flak 28 (Oerlikon)
20 mm Flak 38 L/65, also mounted on Sd.Kfz. 10, 70 and 251/17
20 mm Mountain Flak 38
20 mm Quad Flak 38, also on Sd.Kfz. 7
25 mm Hotchkiss Flak (captured British gun)
30 mm Flak MK 103 on 20 mm Flak 38 mount, also on Sd.Kfz. 70
30 mm Quad Flak MK 103/38

An 88 mm Flak battery of six guns. (BA)

Medium Flak

37 mm Flak 18 (usually on 37 mm Flak 36 mount)
37 mm Flak 36/37, also on Sd.Kfz. 6 and 7/2
37 mm Flak 43, also on Sd.Kfz. 7/2
37 mm Twin Flak
37 mm Flak-Breda
37 mm Flak M 39a (captured Russian gun)
40 mm Flak Bofors L/60 (captured gun)
47 mm Flak Skoda (Austrian/Czech)
50 mm Flak 41

Heavy Flak

75 mm Flak L/60 (leftovers)
75 mm Flak M17/34, M36, M33, M30 (captured French gun)
76.2 mm Flak M31 (captured Russian gun, sometimes bored out to 88 mm)
76.2 mm Flak M38 (captured Russian gun, sometimes bored out or rebarreled to 88 mm)
83.5 mm Flak 22 (Czech, made by Skoda)
85/88 mm Flak M39 (captured Russian gun, bored out to 88 mm)
88 mm Flak 18 L/56
88 mm Flak 18 on six-wheeled chassis with two-axle drive by VOMAG (only for Abt. I./42 mot. s.)
88 mm Flak 36/37
88 mm Flak 37 (18/36)/41
88 mm Flak 41 (also 88 mm Flak 42 by Krupp)
88 mm Flak 41 L/71 (also 88 mm Flak 42 by Krupp)
90 mm Flak M39 (captured French gun)
94 mm Flak M39 Vickers (captured British gun)
105 mm Flak 38 and 39
128 mm Twin Flak 40/44 on Flak turrets

The 15 mm Flak guns developed by the Krupp and Rheinmetall firms were only developed as prototypes, by Krupp as "Device 50 and 60" and by Rheinmetall as "Device 55 and 65", and never went into series production.

Flakpanzer

20 mm Flak 38 on P38 (Cezch) tank chassis
20 mm Quad Flak 38 on Panzer IV chassis ("Möbelwagen")
20 mm Quad Flak 38 on Panzer IV chassis (Sd.Kfz.116/1) "Wirbelwind", 1944
30 mm Twin Flak MK 103/38 on Panzer IV chassis, "Kugelblitz"
30 mm Quad Flak MK 103/38 on Panzer IV chassis, "Zerstörer 45"
37 mm Flak 43 on Panzer IV chassis, "Möbelwagen"
37 mm Panzerflak 43 L/60 with Panzer IV chassis (Sd.Kfz. 116/1), improved with armor plate as "Ostwind"
37 mm Twin Flak on Panzer IV chassis (Sd.Kfz. 163), as "Ostwind II" (Pz.IV/J)
37 mm Twin Flak on Panzer IV chassis, "Wirbelwind II"

These anti-aircraft tanks saw service at the front only in small series, if at all.

Heaviest Flak

Anti-aircraft guns of 210 mm and 240 mm never got beyond the planning stage. Their further development was stopped at the highest level.

Work on an anti-aircraft rocket was carried out at the testing institute in Peenemünde. But the construction of V1 and V2 rockets was always given higher priority from above, so that no Flak rockets had seen service when the war ended.

The variety of the Flak weapons used shows on the one hand that improving their quality and performance became necessary during the war, but on the other hand, the use of the numerous captured weapons shows that the production of German weapons could not fully meet needs.

Flak in Action

Within the scope of this book it is not possible to enumerate all the countless, often decisive, uses of Flak weapons against air and ground targets on all fronts. Yet their hard fight, eventually against a more powerful opponent, will be shown here and particularly documented in the following pictures.

In Poland

During the eighteen-day Polish campaign from September 1 to 18, 1939, only limited Flak action against enemy air attacks took place, since the Polish air forces had already been destroyed on the ground by the German Luftwaffe. On the other hand, the Flak guns were often used successfully, for the first time, in ground combat, because of their good ballistic performance, in battles around Graudenz, Warsaw, and on the Narev Line.

Flak guns were used only rarely against air targets during the Polish campaign, since the Polish air forces were quickly destroyed on the ground by German dive bombers. Here a 20 mm Flak 30 is seen in one of the few Polish actions against air targets. (BA)

An 88 mm Flak gun in action against ground targets. (BA)

At the beginning of the war, camouflaging the guns often went too far. This camouflage was certainly a hindrance in fast action. (BA)

The "Dora" gun, recognizable by the "D" on the recuperator, in action against ground targets. The shot has been fired. The officers and men wait to see what effect it has. At the right are camouflaged chassis of Special Trailer 201. (BA)

This camouflaged 88 mm Flak 36, towed by a Medium Towing Vehicle 8 t (Sd.Kfz. 7), is advancing in Poland. (BA)

A position change for an 88 mm Flak 18 in Poland in September. The gun is already lifted. Now the side spars on the cross mount are being folded up alongside the gun and attached there. The unused ammunition is loaded into the towing tractor. (BA)

In Denmark, Norway and Finland

At first, only a few Flak units took part in the occupation of Denmark and Norway. Later, not only naval Flak but also Luftwaffe Flak units came to protect several Norwegian fjords, in some of which ships of the German Navy were kept, and several cities with important industrial facilities. Thus, the Soviet air forces suffered heavy losses in their attacks on Kirkenes, Vadso and the area around Petsamo. Light Flak platoons successfully supported the "Dietl Group" during its defensive actions in the Narvik area. All the units that saw service in the far north, to Murmansk, did their work under the most severe climatic conditions. In the northern area minus Denmark, but including Finland, in 1944, 126 heavy and 80 light or medium Flak batteries of the Luftwaffe saw service. Along with fighter planes, naval Flak and on-board weapons, they were able to shoot down 570 enemy aircraft from July 4, 1944 to April 24, 1945.

This 105 mm Flak 38 is seen in a well-built position in Norway. (BA)

An 88 mm Flak gun in position on the Danish coast, photographed on April 22, 1940. (BA)

A 105 mm Flak battery in Norway in 1941. Shot values were transmitted from the Command Device 36 or 40 by the Transmission Device 30 to the indicator lights on the right side of the gun, showing elevation and traverse. The transmission cable from the distributor box in the center of the battery runs from the right edge of the picture to the gun position. In the right background is another gun of this battery. (BA)

The crew of this 88 mm battery lived in dugouts covered by tent canvas. The smokestack in the foreground indicates that bunker ovens were inside. (BA)

A sentry could stand the cold of the north only when wrapped in a heavy fur coat. In the left background is the snow-covered Command Device 40 of this 88 mm Flak battery. (BA)

Rough winter duty in northern Finland. (BA)

The 88 mm Flak 18, weighing 7.2 tons, caved in the shoulder of this road near Bardenfoss, Norway.

While the German soldiers use a rope to try to keep the gun from tipping over, Norwegians watch, probably with malicious joy.

A 20 mm Flak 30 position in the far north of Norway.

The crew of this 20 mm Flak 38 stand ready to meet the enemy on the coast of Norway in 1943. (BA)

Winter in Finland. The crew of this shielded 20 mm Flak 38 have only a short day before the long winter night falls. (BA)

Wrapped in a sheepskin coat, this sentry stands by a 20 mm Flak 38 on the ice-cold Norwegian coast. The weapon is already loaded with a 20-round flat magazine. Instead of the otherwise customary Flak Sight 38, this gun has a Lineal Sight 21 with a glass lens. (BA)

The use of the sensitive command devices was often problematic in the cold northern winter. This Kdo. Ger. 40 could be heated by a burner installed under the traversing apparatus and covered with canvas. (BA)

In the West

In the western campaign, the Ist and IInd Flak Corps were advanced. To protect the Army's attacking units and the armored units that quickly penetrated the enemy lines from high- and low-level attacks in quick alteration with ground combat against bunkers and tanks, repeated position changes of the individual Flak batteries were often necessary. For example, the I.II covered a total of 2400 km in advances during the western campaign between May 20 and June 24, 1940, and fought from 40 to 50 firing positions, which often had to be created with fatiguing trench-digging. Often, too, individual 88 mm Flak guns saw action as "working guns" (later, in Russia, they were known as "Flak-combat troops") in the foremost lines, to fight down nests of opposition, tank attacks or bunkers. Here the 88 mm Flak achieved very good effects with its armor-piercing shells. Usually just a few shots were sufficient to put the crews in a bunker or tank out of action with a direct hit, by using shells that exploded inside. The most effective shot range for this was up to 2000 meters, meaning that the gun had to be moved forward to such a distance, into a covered firing position. Because of its size, this often could only be done at night. In this way, the citadel of Boulogne was attacked by 88 mm Flak at the closest range. In the Army, the 88 mm Flak was considered the only weapon that could penetrate the armor of the heaviest French and British tanks. The light Flak guns had success against tanks only by firing on their tracks and visors. Because of the ground use of the Flak guns, it had become necessary to equip the guns with protective shields.

The light Flak gun on a self-propelled mount was at an advantage over the other light weapons thanks to its great mobility and immediate readiness to fire. Its great height when mounted on a vehicle was its greatest disadvantage.

This 20 mm Flak 30 secures a road on the advance to Paris. (BA)

On July 10, 1940, the Commanding General of the lst Flak Corps reported that his units had destroyed:
372 aircraft shot down from the air
252 aircraft destroyed on the ground (some captured unharmed)
47 tanks
30 bunkers
1 warship

The IInd Flak Corps reported that it had destroyed:
214 aircraft shot down
284 tanks

17 forts and armored positions
7 transport ships

Such reports of success made it clear that the Flak gun was more and more recognized as a multipurpose weapon. For that reason, during the planning and preparation for Operation "Sealion", the landing on the British Isles, Flak combat troops were included for artillery support of the army units and protection of the embarking harbors. Operation "Sealion", as is well known, was first postponed by the Führer's orders, and finally given up altogether, on account of Operation "Barbarossa", the attack on Russia.

Barbed wire secures this 88 mm Flak battery on the Atlantic coast from surprise attacks by partisans and landing troops. (BA)

The Flak batteries on the Atlantic coast had to fight off not only attacking enemy aircraft but also approaching sea targets. (BA)

Attacking bombers are fired on by the 88 mm Flak guns in a well-built position on the Atlantic coast.

Quickly mobile 105 mm railroad Flak batteries were also ready for action on the Atlantic coast. (BA)

The numerous rings on the gun barrel show how successful this 88 mm battery has been in action.

To attack heavy French tanks and bunkers, 88 mm Flak guns were turned into anti-tank guns, with a larger shield closed over the barrel. The shortened spars could be folded down from the chassis to the ground. This gun was used by I.R. 51 in the 18th I.D. near Dunkerque in May 1940.

This 88 mm Flak 18 is mounted on a 12-ton tractor for use as a tank destroyer as well as against air targets. It saw service with the 8th Heavy Panzerjäger Unit in Poland and France. The engine hood and cab were armored, and a shield protected the gun crew from splinters. The large white German cross on the hood is easy to see.

Four forerunners of the armored artillery on self-propelled halftrack mounts.

This 88 mm Flak 18 is towed by a heavy armored 12-ton tractor (Sd.Kfz. 8). Armor plate protects the gun crew on the tractor as well as the engine and cab.

The 88 mm Flak gun on a 12-ton tractor was mobile and could move quickly, but its size presented an obvious target for enemy fire. This shot-down self-propelled "88" is seen in France in 1940.

This bunker on the Maginot Line was hit by 88 mm Flak fire and taken by German troops in 1940.

After this bunker on the Maginot Line was taken, a German 20 mm Flak gun was positioned on it.

This 50 mm Flak 41 was loaded on a 4.5-ton truck on the French coast. Two jacks were folded down on each side of the truck to steady the rear bed and the gun on it. The range-finder man stood unprotected in his exposed position at the 1-meter range finder. (BA)

The crew of this 50 mm Flak 41 on the channel coast enjoys a little comfort beside their gun, which is ready to fire. (BA)

To protect the locks of St. Nazaire, this 40 mm Flak 28 Bofors stood in its position. Despite the presence of many Army and Navy officers, the airplane spotter calmly watches the skies.

Medium Flak guns also protected the harbor of Cherbourg from low-flying air raids. This 40 mm Flak 28 Bofors has shells loaded from above on a belt, to provide fast firepower.

A 20 mm Flak position above the harbor of Brest. The range-finder operator makes his daily observations with the Em Im R36.

To protect a pontoon ferry on the Somme in 1940, this 20 mm Flak 30 has been moved into position by its crew. (BA)

A 20 mm Flak 30, crewed by men of the General Göring Regiment (RGG), stands on the Channel coast, ready for action. The range-finder operator has his Im R36 set up ready for use on a shoulder rack.

This 20 mm Flak 30 position was in the dunes of the Belgian North Sea coast in 1940-41.

The crew of a 20 mm Flak 38 quad is ready for action on the Atlantic coast. The gun was meant to repel not only low-level air raids, but also possible landing attempts. (BA)

In all kinds of weather, a plane spotter was on duty. This one is in a 20 mm Flak position on the Atlantic coast. (BA)

A 20 mm Flak 38 on the captured Polish Armored Train 22, in action against ground targets in France. Behind the gun is an armored turret with a 75 mm tank gun. (BA)

A 20 mm Flak quad protects an express train, here entering a station in Brussels. (BA)

Between the two gun cars for light Flak is an empty flatcar, so the guns on either side will not get in each other's way. The barrel deflector can be seen in the foreground. The crew could enter the car only by using a ladder to climb over the armored double walls. (BA)

All along the Atlantic coast, anti-aircraft searchlights were in use. This 150 cm Sw 37 is being placed in position along the Atlantic Wall, apparently with some difficulty. (BA)

This 150 cm anti-aircraft Searchlight 37 is in position along the Atlantic coast in southern France. On its left side are the large elevation handwheel for the K1 and the receiver for elevation values. (BA)

In the Balkans

Before the eastern campaign began, though, the Balkan campaign against Yugoslavia and Greece took place in 1941, as a flank attack by the British from there was feared in case of an attack on Russia. The action in the Balkans, though, made a six- to eight-week postponement of Operation "Barbarossa" necessary, with ominous results. While the Yugoslavian troops had already capitulated on April 17, 1941, the war against Greece turned out to be harder. In the rough mountain country and along the Metaxa Line of fortifications, bravely defended by the Greeks, many Flak units were involved in hard fights. It was particularly the Flak combat troops that destroyed numerous bunkers and tanks with direct fire, and thus opened

the way for the advancing mountain troops. On May 2, 1941, this campaign was ended. As of May 1943, the air situation over Greece became more serious, so that strentghening the anti-aircraft forces to secure airfields and important railroad lines, such as Saloniki-Athens, became necessary. After the collapse in the southern sector of the eastern front in 1944 and the fall of Romania and Bulgaria, the German positions in Greece had to be evacuated. In heavy withdrawal combat with heavy losses, the Flak units drew back, along with other Wehrmacht units, through the mountainous landscape of the Balkans. Exposed to constant air attacks and threatened by partisans, their survivors, unless they were not scattered in ground combat, reached the defensive line of the Hungarian-Croatian border.

This 88 mm Flak gun, towed by an 8-ton KM medium tractor with long halftracks, leaves the readiness area headed for the front lines. (BA)

This 88 mm Flak 36 is being pushed laboriously into its chosen position by manpower. (BA)

As soon as the gun is ready to fire, the enemy position on the hill is fired on. The K2 views the target with his ground-target telescope through the window in the shield. With his left hand he operates the traversing drive. The loose indicator is activated via a rod by the aiming-angle drive, which he operates with his right hand. The elevation gunner, K1, sets the fixed indicator with the help of the elevating gear so that it agrees with the loose indicator.

Particularly on the Metaxa Line, a Greek chain of fortifications, the 88 mm Flak gun often had to fire on ground targets. Here the 88 mm Flak is firing on a mountain position. (BA)

The shot has landed. The recoiling barrel has brought the piston rod visible over it, along with the piston of the pneumatic recuperator, back with it. The air thus compressed in the air chamber relaxes again after the conclusion of the recoil, and pushes the brake fluid, which has flowed in, into the recuperator cylinder. (BA)

After the shot, the empty cartridge case is removed. (BA)

An 88 mm Flak 18 and its tractor pass a Flak position on their way to the front. (BA)

Here a veteran crew has taken up a position with their "88". The many rings on the barrel and the good camouflage show that they are veterans. (BA)

Only in particularly critical situations could the 88 mm Flak be fired sideways while on its chassis. Here stability is attained by putting pieces of wood under the folded-down side spars. (BA)

In the Balkans, partisan attacks took many lives. Here an 88 mm Flak 18, pulled by an 8-ton tractor (Sd.Kfz. 7), passes a fallen messenger and his horse. The crewmen on the tractor are ready to use their carbines against a possible surprise attack. (BA)

This 20 mm Flak quad on a self-propelled mount is in action during an attack. The mount was dug in somewhat, so that the crew and their gun did not stand too high on the "serving tray". (BA)

A 20 mm Flak quad in action in Greece. The ammunition man hands the loader the flat magazines holding 20 rounds each. (BA)

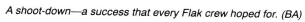

A shoot-down—a success that every Flak crew hoped for. (BA)

Such 20 mm Flak positions in the trackless mountains of the Balkans were very hard to reach and could often be supplied only with the help of mules. (BA)

This 20 mm Flak battery changes positions in a rather unusual way, heading for its new position with the help of an oxcart. (BA)

A 37 mm Flak 36 in action. (BA)

On this eight-ton tractor, which has its engine hood and cab armored, a 37 mm Flak 36 stands ready for action.

An unhitched 37 mm Flak 18.

This armored eight-ton tractor with a 37 mm Flak 36 carries the men's baggage and pulls a two-wheeled ammunition tractor.

The people stand silently at the edge of the street and watch the German 20 mm Flak quads on armored 8-ton tractors drive by.

In this train, a Gun Wagon 1 (E) with a 20 mm Flak 38 is included for protection against partisan attacks and low-flying planes.

In North Africa

In North Africa, Italian troops went into battle against British units on September 13, 1940. But since this attack soon came to a standstill and appeared to be leading to a catastrophic end for the Italians, the German leadership decided to intervene and assist them. On February 11, 1941, the advance units of the German Afrika-Korps, under the command of General Rommel, landed in Tripoli. They were very soon followed by Flak Regiments 102 and 135, which formed the backbone of the action along with the armored units in both the attack phases and the withdrawal. The fast Flak units, often fighting in the front lines and supporting the Army units as "firemen", stood out particularly. For example, only a few of the many antries were cited as focal points. Thus, in the "Battle of Sollum" at the Egyptian border, more than eighty British armored vehicles were shot down by the I./33 in a tank battle on June 16-18, 1941. Names like Tripoli, Marsa el Brega, where the British Brega position was penetrated on the advance, Benghazi, Tobruk, Badia, and Sidi Barrani on Egyptian soil, were places that every one-time Afrika-corpsman will never forget. In countless other places as well, the Flak guns made the difference in hard fighting. Their often decisive action was even mentioned in the American Secretary of War's situation report of June 30, 1942. The Flak units scored an unusual victory in the fighting around Tobruk, where two British destroyers were sunk by them. The Flak units advancing with the armored units specialized more and more in ground combat, while other units took over the defense of marshy roads, access routes, supply areas, airfields and unloading harbors against air attack. The Flak's success was great, but so were their losses in men and materials on the often coverless expanses of the North African battlefields. In order to strengthen the dwindling Flak units, Hitler ordered, among other things, that ten of the new 88 mm Flak 41 guns of the 0 series be sent ot the Afrika-Korps at once. Rommel was later to be given all the 88 mm Flak 41 guns available in Italy. But only a few of these reached their destination, for most of them were sunk by the enemy while crossing the Mediterranean. Under the oppressive air superiority of their opponents, and without any significant supply service of their own, the last of the Afrika-Korps, and the Flak units with them, had to lay down their arms in May 1943.

The crew of this 20 mm Flak on heavy personnel car with support axle, from which the wheels have been removed, aims at a ground target in Africa. The crewmen not needed for this action have taken cover. (BA)

During this morning rest stop on an advance in Tunis, some of the crew of this 88 mm Flak 36 still have their overcoats on. They needed them when riding at night on the 12-ton tractor. (BA)

This 88 mm Flak 18's crew rides on their 8-ton tractor, as fast as the terrain allows, to their next action on the coast of North Africa. (BA)

An 88 mm Flak in action in Tunis in 1943, apparently firing explosive shells, set with a raised explosion point, at a ground target. The fuse-setter's chair is empty, yet the igniters are being set with the same fixed value in the fuse-setting machine. (BA)

Over the shield of this 88 mm Flak, a very coarse net has been stretched, so camouflage can be attached to it. But on the broad, dry desert of North Africa there is no camouflage material to be found. (BA)

Often the extensive desert flatlands offered no cover at all. Whether tank, gun or truck, all stood unconcealed and visible from afar.

This 20 mm Flak quad's crew is changing positions. The men are just pushing the gun to the truck, which bears the emblem of the Afrikakorps. (BA)

Before changing positions, the shell box is emptied. Apparently its action in this position was only brief, as shown by the few shell casings. The shield still has to be folded back against the gun before the gun is ready to move. (BA)

The dry grass does not offer this 20 mm Flak much cover. (BA)

Here a 37 mm Flak 36 position has been dug laboriously in the stony ground. The upper rim of the pit has been raised a bit with sandbags. The range-finder man carries his 1m R36 Range Finder on a shoulder rack, ready to use, and is measuring the target, while the gun crew is in position, waiting for the command to fire. (BA)

In Italy

After the front in North Africa fell, air attacks by the American USAF and the British RAF against Italy increased greatly. For the long supply routes from the Brenner Pass to Sicily, with many important transit centers, there was not enough Flak protection. Yet in the evacuation of German troops from the island of Sicily to the mainland at the Straits of Messina, the Flak units showed what they could accomplish in mass action. Thirty heavy batteries, in what became known as the "Flak bell of Messina", supplied anti-aircraft protection that let the troops on Sicily leave the island without heavy losses, since the Allied bombers could scarcely penetrate this barrier. On the other hand, the German air forces on the Italian mainland were powerless against the thousand daily enemy flights, so that supplies could usually move only at night, since roads and railways were covered by enemy fighter-bombers, that fired on anything that moved, during the day. Just to protect the important Brenner highway in the late autumn of 1944, 88 heavy batteries and numerous light and medium batteries were on hand, yet they could not hold off the daily attacks by hundreds of bombers and fighters.

This Flak 38 quad is only slightly dug in here in southern Italy. The Special Trailer 52 is already on hand for a quick position change. (BA)

The ground-action shield of this 20 mm Flak quad is camouflaged by all sorts of plants, which were stuck behind the wires provided for that purpose. (BA)

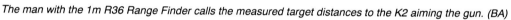

The man with the 1m R36 Range Finder calls the measured target distances to the K2 aiming the gun. (BA)

A 20 mm Flak quad battery changes positions in southern Italy. Pulled by four horsepower, the limbers with the guns hitched to them move to a new position. (BA)

In this only slightly dug-out position, one of the 20 mm Flak quads is being dismounted. The crew also moves the Sd.Ah. 52 out of the gun position. (BA)

This 37 mm Flak 36 is ready for action in southern Italy. The gunner sights the target through the Flakvisier 35. (BA)

It is not easy for the crew of this 20 mm Flak 30 to observe the enemy with the sun in their eyes. (BA)

The aiming gunner of a 20 mm Flak 30 sits behind his weapon. With his right hand he turns the elevation handwheel. Through the hole of the pivoted ring sight he engages the target on the rim of the circle, in the center of which is the target ball. (BA)

The crew of a self-propelled 37 mm Flak 36 changes its gun barrel in a seaport in southern Italy. The old barrel is already removed; the new one lies in its container beside the quay wall. (BA)

The new barrel of the 37 mm Flak 36 is installed. (BA)

88 mm Flak guns in action in Italy. The guns have just fired a volley. (BA)

A German 88 mm Flak crew works hard to build up a position without disturbing their Italian allies. (BA)

This camouflaged 88 mm Flak 18 has taken a defensive position in Italy. Tents provide temporary housing for the crew. (BA)

In the Nettuno area, this 88 mm Flak 18 awaits an American attack in 1944. The battery chief informs the gun leader of the target to be fired on. (BA)

Here an 88 mm Flak gun is lifted from a Flak ferry to the quay by a crane.

This 88 mm Flak 36 is loaded onto a ship in a south Italian port for shipment to Africa.

The guns of this 88 mm Flak battery receive their shot values from the Command Device 36. The values are transmitted over a 108-strand cable, which can be seen at the base of the wall. (BA)

Here a Command Device 40 is being used as a fire-control device. The technical gunner stands in front, in touch with the guns via microphone and earphones. He transmits the commands to fire and operates the fire bell. Behind him are the elevation and traverse gunners, with the range-finder man between them. (BA)

During the Eastern Campaign

At the beginning of the eastern campaign against Russia, there were only thirty motorized units of the First and Second Flak Corps of the Luftwaffe available on the long front. The Army, to be sure, had ten Flak units of its own, but each had only three batteries, and not all of them were ready for action when the campaign began. In all, the number of Flak units soon proved to be much too meager, especially as here, as in all the previous campaigns, they were drawn more and more into ground combat. Above all, it was again the 88 mm Flak guns that saw service successfully against the heavy Russian KW-I, KW-II, T-35 and later T-34 tanks, while the 37 mm Pak guns, sarcastically nicknamed "tank-door-knocking devices" by the troops, could only occasionally score any success with a direct hit to a visor or other weak point.

But there, too, where there were difficulties to be overcome on the advance routes, whether rivers had to be crossed or fortifications had to be fought down, the Flak combat troops or entire Flak batteries led the attack. This, of course, resulted in their use as assault artillery, where the losses of well-trained officers and gun crews were heavy and the guns were lacking for defense against air attacks. The losses were made up by the transfer of active soldiers from Flak batteries in Germany, where they were then lacking to fight off the increasing attacks by enemy bombers and fighter-bombers. The training of Flak combat troops for operations with time limits was expanded and perfected later by the combination of several Flak combat troops into a Flak battle group.

As a rule, a Flak combat troop consisted of one 88 mm Flak, two 20 mm Flak guns, one [p. 69] towing tractor, two Kfz. 81 to tow the 20 mm Flak, and two motorcycles. The personnel included one officer, four NCOs (three gun leaders and one z.b.V.), 22 men and one medic.

In ground combat, the 20 mm Flak was particularly effective against enemy troop concentrations because of its high firepower. Against the slow-flying but heavily armored Russian fighter planes, such as the IL-2 and the IL-17, or "Sewing Machine", they were successful only when armed with a variety of incendiary, explosive and armor-piercing shells. The two following citations are examples of the success of Flak guns in the east. The Ist Flak Corps reported that, for the time between June 22 and mid-September 1941, they destroyed about 300 Russian planes and 3,000

An 88 mm Flak battery rolls along a dusty road in pursuit of the enemy in the central sector of the eastern front in 1941. (BA)

armored vehicles. The war day-book of Flak Regiment 104 records the following scores for the period from June 22, 1941 to April 1, 1942: 252 aircraft shot down, 63 captured on the ground, one destroyed on the ground, 106 tanks and one armored train destroyed, 22 batteries, 19 individual guns, 60 anti-tank guns and 67 grenade launchers destroyed or captured, likewise 288 machine-gun nests, two B-positions, two ammunition dumps and one fuel dump destroyed, 159 motor vehicles and other vehicles destroyed, 41 captured, 2,934 prisoners taken. In 500 ground-combat actions, numerous infantry forces were shattered or wiped out in attacks or concentrations. The reports of other Flak regiments that saw service in Russia show similar success. To the bitter end, there was no decisive combat action in the east where the Flak units did not take part in ground combat in some way, as in 1942, in the large-scale combat in the southern sector, around Voronesh, in the Don oxbow, around Stalingrad, to the peninsula of Crimea and the sea lane by Kertch. Here, in January 1943, a "Flak bell" similar to the afore-mentioned one at Messina, was set up successfully by the 9th Flak Division to protect the supply lines to the Kuban bridgehead. In the north, too, there were several Flak divisions near Leningrad (now St. Petersburg), on the Volkov and Lake Ilmen. At Rshev and in the space around Orel, they took part in the defensive action. It is impossible to mention the countless actions of the Flak troops on the fronts from northern Finland to the Black Sea and the Caucasus within the scope of this book. They often formed the backbone of the "wandering pockets" or so-called "fixed locations" that were surrounded by the enemy at times. After the defeat of the 6th Army, with whose fate that of several Flak units was linked, in Stalingrad, it was often the Flak batteries who were the last to detain the enemy to allow other troop units to withdraw to new positions. In May 1944, what remained of the 9th Flak Division met its end on the Chersones peninsula while protecting the embarkation of what remained of the 17th Army. Until then, this 9th Flak Division had shot down 265 airplanes and 189 tanks in the heavy fighting on the Crimean peninsula.

This 20 mm Flak 38 quad sees service during the second Russian winter. (BA)

From the end of 1943 on, Russian air attacks on the combat areas increased. In the central sector alone, there was a daily average of some 1,090 day and 180 night flights recorded for a month in mid-1944. But since the German Flak units were needed more and more for ground combat, they were only rarely available for anti-aircraft defense. Even so, the flak guns shot down 369 Soviet aircraft in August 1944.

The Army Group North was cut off from East Prussia until October 1944 and pushed together in Courland. In this pocket, the Army, Navy and Luftwaffe Flak units shot down 110 enemy planes from October 29 to November 7, 1944. But here too, the Flak units were chiefly active in ground combat. Of the desperate defensive efforts toward the end of the war, only the costly combat in East Prussia, cut off from the Reich, and the attempt to stabilize the Oder front against the Russians with the help of Flak units can be mentioned. For this, 456 heavy and 186 light and medium Flak batteries were taken away from Reich air defense up to February 26, 1945, and thrown into the Oder front

against the Russian advance. Since many Flak batteries were not motorized, transporting them was often done in adventurous ways. Standing on makeshift mounts, the guns were brought to the front by wood-gas vehicles, fire trucks, moving vans, even on "Bolles" milk wagons, and on account of their immobility, they were often wasted senselessly at the front. From January 12 to the end of February 1945, 41 heavy and 35 light or medium batteries were lost in combat against the Russians on the Oder front, after 135 tanks and 100 aircraft had been shot down by them.

While the Russians reached the Oder and prepared to attack Berlin, many units of the Wehrmacht fought desperately in Silesia and Hungary, suffering heavy losses against opponents far superior in men and materials. Although 153 aircraft and 115 tanks were destroyed by German fighter planes and Flak guns in Hungary from October 29 to November 29, 1944, these losses had no negative effect on the enemy attacking strength. Thus, even the heroic efforts of all troop units could not prevent the catastrophic defeat with all its results.

Shot after shot exits the barrels of this 88 mm Flak battery, fired at a Russian position. (BA)

This 20 mm Flak 30 was used to protect the Volga bridge at Rshev in 1942.

The crew of this 20 mm Flak 38 takes part in ground combat to fight off a Russian attack. (BA)

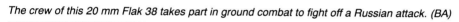

This 20 mm Flak 30 protected the makeshift bridge over the Njemen (Memel) river near Prienai in 1941.

This 20 mm Flak gun's crew had time to dig their self-propelled mount in far enough so the gun had an open field of fire above the wall of earth.

A 20 mm Flak on a truck of the General Göring Regiment (RGG) in Russia in 1941.

A 20 mm Flak on a one-ton tractor of the II./7th Führer Flak Unit fighting among the houses in Krasny-Partisan near Millerovo. The battery belonged to a battle group that was to break the ring around Stalingrad from the Donetz, was surrounded in Millerovo, but was able to break free to the west.

A 20 mm Flak 30 in action in the central sector of the eastern front, protecting a railroad track from partisan attacks in the winter of 1943-44. (BA)

From a Flak 38 position, two sentries observe the field before them. One uses 10x80 searchlight aiming glasses in place of a telescope. (BA)

A position of the so-called Horse Flak in the Pripyet Marshes near Luninieo in 1942. The platforms for the gun position and the tent providing quarters for the men stand on piles in the swamp. (BA)

This 20 mm Flak 38 of the RGG, on a one-ton tractor, and its trailer for ammunition and baggage, are slightly dug in on the HKL.

A 20 mm Flak crew takes a break. They have kept their rations in the spare-barrel box on the rear of the 8-ton tractor (Sd.Kfz. 7) that serves as the gun's self-propelled mount. (BA)

The cab and grille of this light one-ton towing tractor (Sd.Kfz. 10/4) are lightly armored. As the marks on the shield show, this 20 mm Flak gun and its crew have been very successful. (BA)

On this Reichsbahn Gun Wagon I (E) in a 20 mm Flak 28 "Oerlikon". The crew can get into the wagon only by using a ladder.

The armored and makeshift armored trains, most of which saw service in Russia, also carried light Flak guns. This 20 mm Flak is in an armored position on a makeshift gun car of Armored Train No. 1 in Russia in the winter of 1941-42.

This 20 mm Flak 38 quad served in Russia on Armored Train 51 in 1942-44. During transit, muzzle protectors were put on the guns to keep dirt out. The armor plates of the shield were folded up.

The crew of this 20 mm Flak 30 did not have much space on Armored Train 4.

Despite ice-cold weather in February 1943, this 20 mm Flak twin had at least one sentry while Armored Train 24 was moving.

A 20 mm Flak quad on Uniform Armored Train PZ 63. (BA)

A 37 mm Flak position near Narva in the winter of 1943-44. The gun is surrounded by a wall of snow, ice and railroad ties, since it was impossible to dig into the hard-frozen ground. (BA)

To protect this railroad line in the central sector in Russia, especially from partisan attacks, this 37 mm Flak position was set up. A service train brings food to the crew. (BA)

A 37 mm Flak 36 protects a bridge in Russia. A flat magazine with five rounds lies ready on the loading table of the gun. (BA)

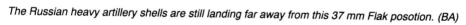

The Russian heavy artillery shells are still landing far away from this 37 mm Flak posotion. (BA)

An 88 mm Flak and a 37 mm Flak 18 in waiting positions. The range-finder man carries the shoulder rack for the 1m R36 Range Finder on his shoulders, ready to use it. Near the 37 mm Flak gun there lies a spare barrel, ready for a quick change.

A self-propelled 37 mm Flak gun, with a trailer for ammunition and the crew's baggage, advances in Lithuania.

These two pictures (BA) show the use of the 37 mm stick grenade by the 9th Co., Light Flak Unit 411 (Sf), near Partischi in March 1944. After the muzzle brake was unscrewed, the stick grenade was placed in the muzzle. Since the best range against tanks was 130 meters and closer, the first shot had to destroy the target. A second shot was scarcely possible because of the time it took to reload. The effect of the head of the stick grenade was similar to that of the "Panzerfaust" or "Panzerschreck".

During the mud season of 1943, this 12-ton DB 10 tractor (Sd.Kfz. 8), towing an 88 mm Flak gun, makes its way through deep mud near Krivoy-Rog.

Fording a stream caused no difficulties for this 12-ton tractor with an 88 mm Flak 18 in tow. The shape of the front fender suggests an older model of Sd.Kfz. 8.

Position change! The 12-ton tractor has backed up to the gun position to tow the 88 mm Flak out. The crewmen load their baggage from the tent onto the tractor. (BA)

Villagers help the gun crew push their 88 mm gun into a new position. (BA)

July 1942: between Kastoronye and Stary Oskol, a 12-ton heavy tractor quickly tows an 88 mm Flak 37 to the front. (BA)

The "Emil" gun of a Flak battery fires on an enemy bridgehead.

Here the chief of an 88 mm Flak battery reports to the unit commander on the situation. (BA)

Despite the canvas cover, it was ice-cold on the tractor on the road. Every brief rest stop was used to warm up by moving around. Russia, February 1944. (BA)

This 88 mm Flak gun's fire on an enemy position is obviously successful, as the battery officer and the gun crew can observe. (BA)

The 88 mm Flak is dismounted, its chassis camouflaged near the gun. From a raised position, a sentry searches the wide flatlands with the help of searchlight binoculars. (BA)

The 88 mm Flak fires on enemy troop concentrations east of Mavrochori.

The shot recoil has pushed the barrel and breech far back, pulling the piston rod of the recuperator with it. The gun leader observes the effect of the shot through binoculars. (BA)

The breech and indicator lights of this 88 mm Flak are still protected from the cold by coverings until the crew makes the final preparations for firing.

South of Lake Ilmen in the Starya Russa area, the crew of an 88 mm Flak gun fires on an enemy tank attack. (BA)

While the crew of a Panzer III waits for the order to fire, the 88 mm Flak fires on the enemy position. (BA)

Russia, summer 1942: Tank alarm! The gun is fired directly from the chassis (an exception), only the spars being folded down and braced with wooden blocks. (BA)

Instead of white paint, this 88 mm Flak gun has been camouflaged for the winter with white cloth. The recuperator has been wrapped in straw to keep it from freezing.

This 88 mm Flak has been positioned on a four-axle SS railroad car. The Cyrillic lettering on the side suggests that it a captured Russian car fitted with standard-gauge wheels. The partially folding sidewalls have been raised on both sides for protection, and the space inside filled with sandbags. (BA)

It appears that two 88 mm Flak guns have been mounted over the double axles of an SS flatcar. The sideboards have been folded down so the spars of the guns can be used; now the spars stick out over the sides of the car.

This 88 mm Flak battery, seen near Rshev in January 1942, has been mounted temporarily on X-wagons (two-axle flatcars). The car in front carries two 20 mm Mountain Flak 38 for use against low-flying planes. They have fixed shields and stand on three legs on a metal mount.

An 88 mm Flak position near Narva in April 1942. In the middle (at left in the picture) is the Auxiliary Command Device 35 (Kdo.Hi.Ger. 35). The Em 4m (R) 40 range finder is on a standard at right. Searchlight direction glasses have been set up between them as an aiming telescope. Behind them is the large case in which the range finder is carried.

The heavy case holding the 4-meter range finder is loaded onto the troop's truck (Kfz. 4) by the command-device crew. Two rails on its bed let the case slide on and off. The men have their seats along the sidewalls of the truck. (BA)

With the help of the panoramic telescope on Command Device 36, the troop leader carries out the daily aiming test with the guns. The man at right maintains telephone contact with the guns. On the front of the device are the ignition drum at left and the barrel-elevating drum at right; between them is the box with the knobs for adjustment. The two arms with the balls at the ends helped to support the canvas cover. (BA)

The Command Device 36 changes its position. The range finder has been removed already. Now the cover is pulled over the device. Russia, winter 1942-43. (BA)

In the German War Zone

The activity of Flak units in the Reich at the beginning of the war consisted mostly of waiting for enemy flights. Endless times of readiness to fire, during which the crews had to stay right with their guns and equipment, alternated with aiming and range-finding drills, using their own airplanes, which flew definite courses for targeting practice. Only now and then did the British fly in at that time, at first only in daylight, and at most only with a group of three planes, to attack German industrial areas. Since they suffered heavy losses from fighter planes and Flak guns, they began to attack at night. Fighting them was only possible through the use of searchlights, supported by listening devices, the ring-funnel direction hearers. But the lights could only be used in clear weather, and only then was optical targeting with Flak command devices possible. Only with the later use of radio targeting devices (FuMG) could the Flak units successfully locate enemy planes without optical targeting. But at first it was only possible to fight the bombers, which now came more often and could not be spotted by searchlights on dark and murky nights, by firing ammunition-wasting barrage fire. In 1940-1942 there were ever Luftwaffe barrage-fire batteries formed, without command devices, to prevent the approaching enemy planes from pinpoint bombing. These batteries were usually equipped with captured guns, some of which were scrapped after their barrels were worn or the captured ammunition was used up.

At this point it is surely interesting to mention the success of the Flak units for the period from September 1, 1939 to October 31, 1941. Destroyed by the Flak guns were: 5,381 airplanes, 1,253 bunkers, 34 armored forts, 1,930 armored vehicles, 279 battery positions, 2,901 artillery guns, anti-tank guns and grenade launchers, 5,631 machine-gun nests, 5,024 trucks, 119 columns, 55 freight trains, 4 destroyers, 19 warships, 16 transport ships, 32 ammunition dumps and one citadel.

The "Berta" gun of the 1./407, a 105 mm Flak battery located in the vicinity of Büderich, near Düsseldorf, in 1940-41, in night action against British bombers.

Toward the end of 1942, more than 700 heavy and some 400 light and medium Flak batteries stood ready to defend the Reich area. At this time, the first large-scale air raids on Cologne and Essen took place. It was mainly the inner cities that were hit. Heavy mine bombs, so-called "block-busters", vast numbers of stick incendiary bombs and hard-to-extinguish liquid incendiary bombs had demoralizing effects in these and all later bombings. Since America had entered the war in December 1941, the air attacks against Germany became even heavier. While the British usually attacked easily inflammable city centers at night (note the memoirs of Air Marshal Harris, Chief of the British Bomber Command), the targets of the USAF in their daylight raids were mostly militarily important targets such as key industries, U-boat support points, shipyards, powerplants and transport systems. These attack tactics forced many Flak batteries in overflight areas to be on an alarm basis day and night. Impressive defensive statistics were reported when, in a large-scale USAF raid on the ball-bearing works in Schweinfurt on October 15, 1943, when 62 of the 228 attacking planes were shot down by fighters and Flak guns, and only 28 returned to their bases without considerable damage.

An 88 mm Flak battery fires salvo after salvo at the approaching planes.

As can be read in enemy sources, the German anti-airfraft defenses were feared by the RAF, as also by the USAF as of 1942. This resulted in the enemies changing their attacking tactics; now the bombs were dropped from tight waves of bombers at altitudes of 5000 to 9000 meters, so that only a very short effective defensive period remained, particularly for the 88 mm Flak. The 105 mm, the few 128 mm and the new 88 mm Flak 41 reached these heights better. In order to keep on using the 88 mm Flak effectively, the already mentioned large batteries were formed. These were meant to apply a lot more firepower against the enemy in the short time they had to fire on targets. Three or four 88 mm batteries with six guns apiece were set up in the usual rectangular pattern with a radius of some 30 meters around the command device in the center. In a bunker, the tactical gunner had his position with the telephone switchboard and data evaluation. Two FuMG were separated, assigned to overlapping search sectors. The German anti-aircraft defenses suffered a serious setback on July 24, 1943, when in a series of day and night raids on Hamburg, "windows", called "Düppel" by the Germans, were dropped in great numbers, disturbing the radar of the night fighters and Flak guns. These were strips of aluminum foil, half as long as the wavelength of the impulses sent out by the radar, which were interrupted by them. Nothing was left for the Flak guns but scarcely effective barrage fire, so that the British and Americans could target and drop over 10,000 tons of incendiary and explosive bombs with almost no interference.

Although the Flak units were able to report shooting down 8,706 aircraft from the beginning of the war to December 31, 1942, they could still not prevent the public's opinion of them to be less than flattering. Despite an often self-sacrificing fight, the Flak could only rarely hold off the air attacks, growing more numerous since the end of 1942, on the objects they were meant to protect so thoroughly that no bomb damage was done. To be sure, their morale was not shattered despite the heavy losses among the civilian population and the heavy damage to their dwelling areas, especially in the second half of the war, but the people's respect for the Flak disappeared. They were unfairly held responsible for the presumably insufficient defense of the cities, notwithstanding the big talk of the Commander of the Luftwaffe, Hermann Göring, who said they could call him any name they pleased if even one enemy plane appeared over Berlin. The critics completely ignored the fact that the Flak units, particularly in the second half of the war, were facing an enemy who vastly outnumbered them. The enemy attacked with large packs in short periods of time. Thus, there were often more planes in the sky than there were gun barrels ready to attack them from the ground. While hundreds of bombers often flew over a target and dropped their carpet of bombs, the Flak had only minutes to attack a few planes in the packs. Before the target area was reached, they had to fire as many shots as possible at them. This was made harder by the enemy's frequent systematic low-flying or carpet-bombing attacks on the gun positions before their large-scale raids, putting them out of commission or at least dropping "windows" to disturb their radar devices. The heavy batteries tried to attack the low-flying planes not only with their light guns, but also to meet them with close-range fire. To do this, the barrels of the guns were not all pointed the same way, but in a hedgehog pattern, with the barrels pointing to all sides from the center of the battery, and with an elevation of about 20 degress outward. Their close-range ammunition was ready, with fuses set for some 500 meters. Of course their success was meager, but the enemy was scared off and the gun crews did not have to stand helplessly and let the attack proceed over their heads. Despite these difficulties, statistics spoke for themselves [p. 99]. Official British sources state that in 1942 the RAF lost some 1,300 combat planes. According to American statistics, in the period from January 1 to October 31, 1943, 727 "Flying Fortresses" of the USAF did not return and 36% of the returning planes were badly damaged by Flak fire. A further report of the USAF states that, in the period from September 1942 to June 30, 1944, 886 four-engined bombers were shot down by Flak guns over Germany, and 21,459 returned with damage. The high numbers of "merely" damaged aircraft shows that the construction of the American bombers was very sturdy. Many of these badly damaged planes were only able to save themselves by making emergency landings in neutral countries, either Switzerland or Sweden. But such impressive statistics do not disguise the fact that effective protection of the German people could not be provided. It was made even harder by the constant change of attacked targets, which required constant transfers of the Flak batteries. This, though, was not possible, as many German guns were set on immobile mounts, and chassis and motor vehicles were lacking.

Despite heavy anti-aircraft fire, the enemy has dropped his bombs effectively and apparently started a fire. (BA)

As of 1943, the enemy attacked the backward front areas to a greater degree, with low-flying fighter-bomber packs penetrating far into the German hinterlands. At first, troop movements and means of transportation were their targets. Later, their weapons were used on anything that moved on roads, rails and waterways, so that in some areas all transportation broke down during the day. To maintain rail service at least in limited areas, more railroad transport protection Flak batteries (ETr.) were set up. On R-, S- or X- flatcars, crews rode with a 20 or 37 mm Flak, or particularly with quadruple 20 mm Flak guns, to secure important transport and supply trains, as well as passenger trains. These measures were not completely unsuccessful, as shown by a report of ETr. Flak Regiment 159, in which this unit reported its 1000th plane shot down. Though the bombers had a certain respect for the strengthened Flak protection added to railroad trains, the units could scarcely prevent the attacks, which is emphasized in the following daily report of the German Reichsbahn

to the Luftwaffe General Staff on May 21, 194 In this report it is stated dispassionately that the were:

	Dead	Wounded
Engine drivers	5	34
Engine firemen	9	28
Train leaders	-	5
Train conductors	2	7
Switchmen	-	6
Passengers	37	113

Along with these losses, there were 70 unu able and 35 slightly damaged locomotives. On th day, the ETr. shot down three aircraft. Not a da went by on which Mosquito units and other lig fighter planes, which could take off from airfield on the Continent since the successful invasio did not attack transport movements on the trans routes, causing more and more damage to ther Since a barrage of German fighter-bombers wa ruled out for lack of fuel, there was no defense b the transport protection units, which also suffere from lack of personnel.

To protect rail transport, this 20 mm Flak 38 takes its place at the end of the train. The walls of the car are reinforced with wooden planks to protect the gun crew. (BA)

In 1944 the Allied increased their air raids on the fuel industry, vital to the war. In August alone, 26,320 tons of bombs fell on these works. Of the 1,368 four-engine warplanes of the 8th U.S. Air Corps that attacked the powerplant at Pölitz near Magdeburg in June, the German defensive forces shot down 48, and another 468 were damaged, mainly by Flak. Now they paid the price because 140 heavy Flak batteries, including numerous railroad units, and 50 light and medium batteries had been transferred to the invasion front, where they were, of course, also needed urgently, but they were lacking for the defense of the German fuel industry, attacks on which were being increased greatly. The results of these attacks were so drastic that the Reich Minister for Armaments, Sperr, had to report a loss of 90% of aircraft fuel production. In the autumn, increased protection for this vitally needed industry was ordered. For example, up to 700 heavy Flak guns were placed in positions around the Leuna works near Halle, and 800 around the works near Heidebreck in Upper Silesia. This move, of course, was made at the cost of protection around several large cities, from which these batteries had to be taken.

Yet the Flak could record success, even in those difficult times. For example, in an attack by some 240 four-engine American planes on the power station at Pölitz in Langenberg, near Stettin, on October 7, 1944, eighteen planes were shot down in thirteen minutes by 88 and 105 mm Flak, and eight others had to make emergency landings in Sweden because of heavy Flak damage. In similar large-scale attacks by streams of up to 1,000 bombers, heavy destructive fire was used, making great physical demands on the gun crews. On the other hand, though, lack of ammunition resulted in the banning of barrage fire, because the ammunition consumption was too great and success was too meager. Attacks on lone reconnaissance planes were also banned. Groups of planes could only be attacked with a few bursts of fire in favorable areas. This often impelled the civilian population to believe that silence from the Flak guns meant cowardice or incompetence.

The crew of this 88 mm Flak gun, in a trench near Königsberg in 1945, was ready to fire on any enemy attack, with carbines if necessary.

A 20 mm Flak 30 with Flak Sight 35, in firing position. The muzzle-flash damper can be seen clearly.

The crew of a 2 cm Flak 30 in a well-built position, in which the gun stands on a raised podium.

A 20 mm Flak 30 with Flak Sight 35, in firing position. The muzzle-flash damper can be seen clearly.

The lower mount of a 20 mm Flak gun is raised to the top of a factory by means of ratchet cranes, to be united there with the other parts of the gun and put into position.

The light and medium Flak guns were often placed on top of tall buildings (left) or on specially built wooden towers (below) to protect objects. But since they could be swept from their positions by the explosion of large bombs in their vicinity, in the end they were no longer placed on such high places.

A 20 mm Flak 30 crew with a cartridge device in the Ruhr area in 1940. Note the old type of gas mask.

The 20 mm Flak gun could be used against ground targets in a makeshift mount of wood. Used this way, it could fire a quick succession of single shots but no bursts of fire.

A 20 mm Flak crew drilling with their gun in the country. In the foreground, the range-finder man carries his 1m R36 range finder on a shoulder rack, ready for use.

The gun leader and crew of this 20 mm Flak tensely search the skies.

A 20 mm Flak battery is seen sharpshooting at the Babenhausen firing range on July 30, 1942.

For the gun to be ready to fire, the aiming gunner's seat always has to be occupied. Here the le.Hei. 30/X1, a 20 mm Flak quad battery, is ready to fire at the Hindenburg Locks in Anderten, near Hannover.

This 20 mm Flak quad of the le.Hei. 30/X1, is in position at the Hindenburg Locks in Anderten, and being prepared by its crew.

This 20 mm Flak 38 is being used to protect a train. A wall of concrete shields the gun.

The 20 mm Flak quad position on Armored Train No. 67 was very cramped and offered its crew little room to move.

Early in 1942, this train was up graded to become regular Armored Train 51. It carried a 20 mm Flak quad on its gun car.

In Hamburg, Berlin and Vienna, Flak towers were built, on which 105 mm, 128 mm or twin 128 mm Flak guns were mounted. To protect them from low-flying planes, 20 mm Flak quads were positioned on somewhat lower platforms. This picture shows the shot tower in Berlin-Friedrichshain in March 1944.

One of the 20 mm Flak quads stands on a lower platform of the gun tower (G-Turm) in Berlin-Friedrichshain. (BA)

Off Friedrichshafen on Lake Constance, two Reichsbahn train ferries rebuilt into Flak ships were moored through most of the war. Each one carried three 37 mm Flak 36 on bases built for them. The crews had their quarters on the ships. Here the "Argen" lies at anchor. (BA)

One of the 37 mm Flak guns on the "Argen", with its crew, in action. (BA)

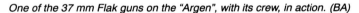

The "Schussen" was built for the German Reichsbahn as a railroad ferry in 1929. After being confiscated by the Navy (or the Luftwaffe?) in 1941 and rebuilt as a Flak ship, it spent most of the wartime at anchor off Friedrichshafen. Note its camouflage paint job. With its two Diesel engines, it could travel at 17.5 kph. It was 54.5 meters long and ten meters wide.

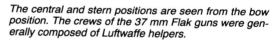

A view from the stern gun position of the "Schussen" toward the central and bow positions with their 37 mm Flak 36 guns.

The central and stern positions are seen from the bow position. The crews of the 37 mm Flak guns were generally composed of Luftwaffe helpers.

This 37 mm Flak 36 was placed on the Kiel Canal to protect a bridge and ship traffic.

The crew of a 37 mm Flak 18 consisted, as can be seen here, of the gun leader with binoculars, the loader and ammunition gunner standing in front of him, the seated aiming gunner, two men using the Flak Sight 33, and the range-finder man with the Em 1m R36. (BA)

The loader of the 37 mm Flak 18 has placed a loading strip of six cartridges on the loading table with his left hand. With his right hand he slowly moves the breech forward, thus pushing the first cartridge out of the loading strip and bringing the breech into its bolted position. (BA)

A 37 mm Flak M39 (captured Russian gun) of the 34./VII Home Flak Battery is ready to fire near Salzburg-Lehn.

A 37 mm twin Flak 43 ready to fire. On the right side of the mount, the shell ejectors of both guns and the shell catcher below can be seen. Sitting at right are the sighting and aiming gunners. The gun leader stands on a platform behind the weapon; to his left, the loader holds a new loading strip ready for the upper gun. (BA)

The loading gunner holds a new cartridge frame, weighing 15 kilograms and holding eight cartridges. (BA)

The crew of a 50 mm Flak 41 cleans their gun. The loader cleans a frame with five cartridges on the platform on which he stands behind the elevation gunner during action. (BA)

A 50 mm Flak 41 in position. The traverse gunner and the sighting gunner are sitting at right near the mechanical clockwork sight. On the left side, the loading gunner has filled the feed with cartridges. The elevation gunner sits behind the shield. (BA)

This 88 mm Flak 18 saw action at Westerland on Sylt on March 6, 1940. (BA)

During the war, more and more 88 mm Flak guns had their chassis and mounts removed for lack of materials, and were mounted rigidly in place. But now the batteries could scarcely be moved. This was a great disadvantage, especially toward the end of the war, since the guns could not be removed when a position was abandoned, but had to be blown up. (BA)

The 12-ton tractor (Sd.Kfz. 8) tows an 88 mm Flak 18 to a new position.

The new position is not easy to reach, and the gun sinks to its axles in the mud.

The new position is firs enclosed by sandbags which also offer protec tion from shell frag ments.

Approaching enemy aircraft were greeted with anti-aircraft fire on the coast.

The "Anton" gun is aimed by using a panoramic scope as the guns and command devices of a battery are set up in the same basic direction. (BA)

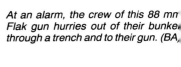

At an alarm, the crew of this 88 mm Flak gun hurries out of their bunker through a trench and to their gun. (BA)

This 88 mm Flak 18 was in position near Frankfurt-Sprendlingen on June 21, 1941.

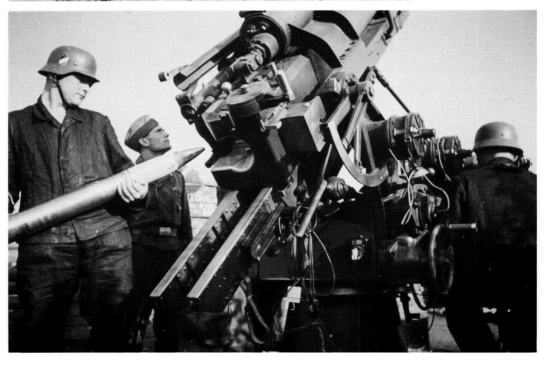

The ammunition gunner of an 88 mm Flak puts a new shell in the second fuse-setter of the fuse-setting machine, while the shell in the first one is being set.

The NCO sits in the traverse gunner's seat of the 88 mm Flak gun by the indicator lights and targeting scope. The elevation gunner's seat beside him is empty. A leather shield has been put over the indicator lights so they can be read better in its shadow.

The "Berta" gun of an 88 mm Flak battery has been loaded onto a flatcar for rail transport, while the gun's chassis is still being loaded. (BA)

The 88 mm Flak 37, dismounted from its chassis, is ready to travel on a flatcar. (BA)

In October 1944, the Reich's air fleet had some 1,500 heavy and 800 light or medium Flak batteries. These were located in large areas around the focal points they defended. But the enemy's tactics of attacking in sectors meant that only a few of the batteries got to fire, and the rest had to watch the attack and do nothing. After the western Allied troops reached the German border in September 1944, the German aircraft reporting stations in the west were lost, so that sufficient warning, not only of the population but also of the flak units near the border, was only rarely possible. Thus, it could happen that air-raid alarms were heard only as the bombs were dropped.

It often looked like this in German cities at night in the last two war years. The enemy used explosive and incendiary bombs to destroy whole districts of cities.

A large 88 mm battery fires on enemy bombers during a night attack.

At night, the bright muzzle flash betrays the Flak positions. This led to the development of Flak ammunition whose powder created less muzzle flash.

Night action for a Flak gun in a position near Sprendlingen in 1940.

A Flak barrel did not always stand up to sustained fire. When a shell exploded prematurely, it could blow part of the barrel off.

The 88 mm Flak guns and their Command Devices 36 and 35 of the four batteries of the lst Unit, Flak Regiment 42 (mot.S.) were the only ones in the Wehrmacht to be carried on six-wheel trucks with two-axle drive, made by the Vogtland Machine Factory (VOMAG). This unit originally saw service as the "Führer's Escort Unit". Because of its great mobility and quick readiness to fire, though, it soon functioned as "firemen" in many parts of Europe, until its fate was sealed in February 1945 in the defense and fall of "Fortress Budapest". Here a gun truck of this unit is seen on the march to Bremen on April 10, 1941.

The gun trucks and two targeting trucks of the 1st Unit, Flak Regiment 42, at an intermediate stop on August 22, 1944, on their way to the "Fu"*hrer's Headquarters South" near Visniova, in the vicinity of Krasnov, Poland.

The "Anton" and "Berta" gun trucks and, at left, the targeting truck o~ the 2./42 (mot.S.).

The 2nd Battery trucks had to drive one after another down a field path to a position near Stettin in October 1941. In front is the targeting truck of B1 with Command Device 36.

One of the 88 mm Fl~ guns on the I./4~ (mot.S.) on a VOMAG gun truck.

This 105 mm Flak battery was set up near the Victory Column on Unter den Linden in Berlin on November 28, 1941, to fire a volley at the state funeral of Werner Mölders. (BA)

The K3 serves as loader on the loading stage of the 105 mm Flak. To his left, the K6 sits at the fuse-setting machine and turns the fuse-setting crank with his right hand.

The 14th Battery of the General Göring Regiment (RGG), a 105 mm Flak battery, is seen on the Flak firing range at Stolpmünde on the Baltic, where the training level of the crew is judged while firing at a moving target.

Since it was harder for a 105 mm Flak gun to change positions than for an 88 mm gun, they were seldom used in ground combat. Here a 105 mm Flak 39 is seen firing at a ground target. (BA)

A heavy 105 mm railroad Flak battery is ready to fire in Air Zone VI.

The loader (K3) of a 105 mm railroad Flak has placed a shell in the holder of the fuse-setting machine. When the fire bell rings, he swings the shell out of the machine into the loading dish. From there it is moved automatically into the barrel. (BA)

A 128 mm Flak 40 of the Neufelder-Koog Battery in Dietmarschen is covered to protect it from the weather in the winter of 1944-45.

A naval helper serves as the traverse gunner at the traversing apparatus of a 128 mm Flak 40 of the Neufelder-Koog Battery.

To the left of the breech of a 128 mm Flak 40 is the fuse-setting machine with its holder and setting head, plus the loading dish.

Naval helpers with a 128 mm Flak 40 of the Neufelder-Koog Battery. The height of the loading stage for the two loading gunners (K3 and K4) was adjusted to the barrel elevation.

The 128 mm Flak guns at Neufelder-Koog were on fixed mounts and not on cross mounts.

This 128 mm Flak 40 is raised to an elevation of 85 degrees.

The following pictures show how the barrel of a 128 mm Flak gun is placed in position. The Barrel Wagon 40 is towed to the mount by a truck. (BA)

Using a winch, the barrel is drawn from the barrel wagon onto the coupling rack, which is laid out in the direction of the gun mount, which is already mounted permanently in position. (BA)

The barrel is drawn into the cradle of the upper mount from the coupling rack. (BA)

It is finished! The barrel of the 128 mm Flak gun is fixed in the cradle, as the first elevation of it shows. (BA)

When the war ended, 34 128 mm Flak twins, 68 barrels in all, stood on Flak towers in Hamburg, Berlin and Vienna. One of these guns is seen here ready for action. (BA)

The twin 128 mm Flak guns have just fired a volley. The powder smoke has not yet dispersed, and the crews are preparing to fire the next volley. (BA)

This 128 mm Flak twin stood on the Heiligengeistfeld flak tower in Hamburg.

The VOMAG targeting truck with the Command Device 36 of the already mentioned 88 mm Flak of the I./42. (mot.S.), with its sideboards folded down to make a larger platform.

The VOMAG targeting truck with its covered Command Device 36 is ready to march. Rolled-up wooden carpets are carried ahead of the front fenders for use on soft ground.

The Command Device 36 on the VOMAG truck is ready for use. The sideboards have been folded down to give the crew more work space.

For lack of a targeting truck, a box containing the Em 4m R (H) range finder and the communication device has been loaded onto a 12-ton tractor (Sd.Kfz. 8). Loading the heavy device was surely not easy. On the trailer is the covered Command Device 36.

Without a command device, effective fire on enemy aircraft by heavy Flak was scarcely possible. Here a crew is seen in action, operating the Command Device 36.

The position of Command Device 40 of the Neufelder-Koog Battery is covered with camouflage nets.

The crew of a Command Device 40 practices aiming at a German plane that provides a target. The bar over the device carries the transmission cable from the Radar Measuring Device (FuMG) 39 T, that can be seen in the background. It provided targeting values when optical targeting with the Kdo.Ger. was not possible. (BA)

This Command Device 40 of the I./407 is ready for action in a position near Büdering, outside Düsseldorf. The raised cable carries targeting values of traverse, elevation and distance to the target from the evaluating device where no visual targeting was possible.

If the radar was lost and no visual targeting was possible, the traverse, elevation and distance values could be received from a neighboring battery. By using the Malsi re-evaluating device, the targeting values for the battery could be worked out and transmitted to the command device by field phone.

Searchlights often received their aiming values for a target from listening devices. Here listening practice is being carried out with an older type of listening device. (BA)

The ring-funnel direction hearer (RHH) of the most frequently used listening device was used until the war's end, despite their short supply, for aiming searchlights, since only a few radar sets were available. Those that were available were needed most by the Flak batteries. (BA)

An RHH of the General Göring Regiment (RGG) is pushed into its new position by manpower after being uncoupled from a tractor. (BA)

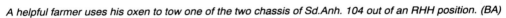

A helpful farmer uses his oxen to tow one of the two chassis of Sd.Anh. 104 out of an RHH position. (BA)

Alarm drill for the crew of a 150 cm Searchlight 37. (BA)

The crew of this 150 cm searchlight was housed in a bunker right beside their equipment. (BA)

Light shines from this 150 cm searchlight. The traverse man in front uses the chest-high control to turn the light. The elevation man stands to the left of the light. (BA)

The searchlights are still seeking their target, although the enemy appears to have dropped incendiary bombs already. (BA)

Along with the beams of light, the tracer ammunition of the light Flak forms strings of pearly light in the night sky. (BA)

Flak Service Personnel in Action

The high personnel losses, particularly on the eastern front, meant that more and more trained Flak officers, NCOs and men were transferred out of the German war zone and sent to the front in Luftwaffe field divisions. As early as September 20, 1942, the Führer ordered training of a "Flak Militia" made up of teenage boys. The drafting of schoolboys, first those born in 1926-27 and later those of 1928-29, only began on January 25, 1943 with a "directive for the war service of German youth in the Luftwaffe". After that, not only schoolboys but also apprentices born in those years were drafted as "Luftwaffe or Navy Helpers", often called "Flak Helpers" as well. At first they were only supposed to serve in Flak batteries in their own school districts. But this changed in 1943. From then on, they saw service without limit in the entire Reich area. Most of them were very enthusiastic about being allowed to contribute to the defense of their homeland, believing they were fulfilling their duty to their people and fatherland, without political ideals playing a role. On the contrary, the influence of the Hitler Youth leaders was generally declined, and the HJ armband to be worn on the left arm of their dress uniforms was often secretly left off. The boys wanted to be regarded not as Hitler Youth members, but as soldiers, which they essentially were. They saw service as operators of the Flak command device, the "Malsi" evaluation device, the radar and the 20 to 128 mm Flak guns, including those in the Flak towers of Hamburg and Berlin. These young people, originally ridiculed as "Flak Babies", proved themselves by their fearless willingness to serve. They did their duty, even when their own positions were attacked and bombs fell around them. As a result, many units suffered heavy losses. On account of the confusion toward the end of the war, no definite loss statistics are extant, so that the number of casualties can never be known.

As of mid-1942, so-called **Alarm Flak Batteries** were established in the German area and the occupied lands in the west. Their service personnel consisted of soldiers from all parts of the Wehrmacht, meaning members of command offices and of large Wehrmacht service facilities, Luftwaffe schools and anti-aircraft troop replacement units who had been trained for Flak artillery by the Luftwaffe.

In addition, **Homeland Flak Batteries** were set up to protect large German industries. Their personnel, along with a small core of trained artillerymen, consisted largely of employees of the large firms. When local air-raid alarms sounded, these Flak men went to their positions on the factory grounds or very near them.

Since the heavy homeland and alarm Flak batteries often lacked fire-control equipment, they could only attempt barrage fire, and so they were also known as "homeland barrage batteries". Their guns were usually captured ones whose combat value was limited, and often served more to calm the population.

Many of the **RAD Flak Batteries** saw service in the occupied western lands and in coastal sectors, and some of them were lost there as immobile batteries. Others were located on the eastern and western German borders in 1944-45, often serving as ground combat batteries, where they held out in hopeless positions knowing they allowed large portions of the population to flee before the enemy arrived.

How precarious the personnel situation was, in the Flak units as elsewhere, in the last two war years is shown by the fact that in German Flak batteries not only "helpers" but also so-called **Flak-V-Soldiers** were used, exchanged for soldiers able to serve at the front. These were usually men with wounds or serious bodily injuries, who may have wanted to do their best but could not be fully capable soldiers for physical reasons. Finally, volunteers from other peoples, such as Walloons and [p. 147] Croats, as well as Russian prisoners of war, known as "**Hilfswillige**", also served in Flak batteries. The latter saw service in 88 mm batteries as ammunition carriers and even as loaders.

In the autumn of 1944, several Flak regiments were formed and specially trained for front service and army support as "**Assault Flak Units**".

They were to serve, as fully motorized units, to protect airfields, but also in ground combat at endangered focal points. These well-trained units enjoyed a good reputation among the troops.

The statistics of October 1944 can serve as an example of the personnel situation of the Luftwaffe Flak artillery. At that time, 600,000 soldiers were in service, plus 520,000 so-called helpers. Of them, some 60,000 were RAD Flak soldiers, 50,000 Luftwaffe helpers, 80,000 Flak defense and Flak-V soldiers, 160,000 female Flak-weapon helpers and RAD women, who served mainly with searchlights and surveillance devices, and 170,000 foreign helpers.

The **Naval Flak** units served not only in antiaircraft defense but also in coastal defense against sea targets, and after the invasion they saw ground-combat service in the defense of focal points and fortifications on the Channel and Atlantic coasts, as well as in the defense of harbors along the Baltic coast as far as Memel.

It should be noted that the **Waffen-SS** set up their own Flak defense units, which took place chiefly in ground action.

The young Luftwaffe helper (Lw.H.) learns to move the ammunition of the 105 mm Flak from the fuse-setter into the loading dish by hand. (BA)

Here an Lw.H. serves as K1 at the elevating control of a 105 mm Flak, apparently steering its fluid drive according to telephoned values, for he is wearing a headset. (BA)

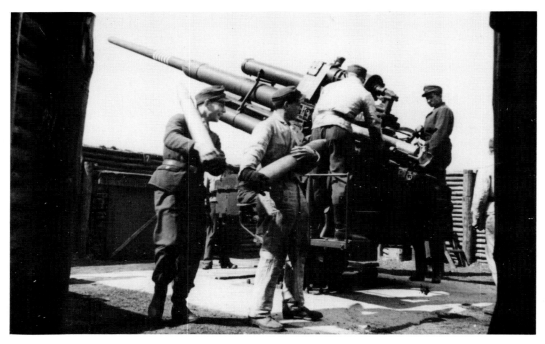

Some of this 105 mm gun crewmen are Luftwaffe helpers. (BA)

Luftwaffe helpers were not supposed to be used as ammunition gunners, but this rule was broken when manpower was lacking. Though it was hard work, carrying ammunition was regarded as an honor. (BA)

Aircraft recognition training for a 105 mm Flak battery. the Flak NCO uses a model to show the recognizable features of an enemy bomber type. (BA)

This 105 mm Flak battery is being taken over by the Reich Work Service (RAD). A Flak NCO explains the loading procedure to an RAD man.

Home Flak batteries, beyond a small cadre of Flak soldiers, were generally recruited from the staffs of large industrial firms. Their gun positions were on the factory grounds. This 20 mm Flak 30 belonged to the 5th Home Flak Battery and was used to protect the Leitz firm in Wetzlar.

The crewmen of the 5th Home Flak Battery were employees of the Leitz firm in Wetzlar. They and their 20 mm Flak 30 are seen here on the Babenhausen firing range.

The guns of the Heavy Home Flak Battery 230/VII were manned mostly by Luftwaffe helpers. This is the crew of the "Anton" gun, a captured Russian 85 mm gun bored out to take the German 88 mm caliber.

The 230/VII Home Flak Battery saw action at Schnetzenhausen near Friedrichshafen, and suffered heavy losses in the bombing of the Dornier works on August 9, 1944. Here the "Friedrich" gun position is seen after the attack. Four of its crew were killed and two wounded.

The "Dora" gun was hit hardest. The eleven-man crew was lost to a direct hit in the gun position. All the ammunition in the bunkers also exploded. Three active soldiers and 23 Luftwaffe helpers of this battery lost their lives in this attack.

Luftwaffe helpers pose for a photograph during training on a 20 mm Flak 30. In everyday service, the Hitler Youth armbands were not worn; they were required only for parades, though secretly removed by many.

Luftwaffe helpers are being trained to use ring-funnel direction hearers (above) and 150 cm searchlights (below). (BA)

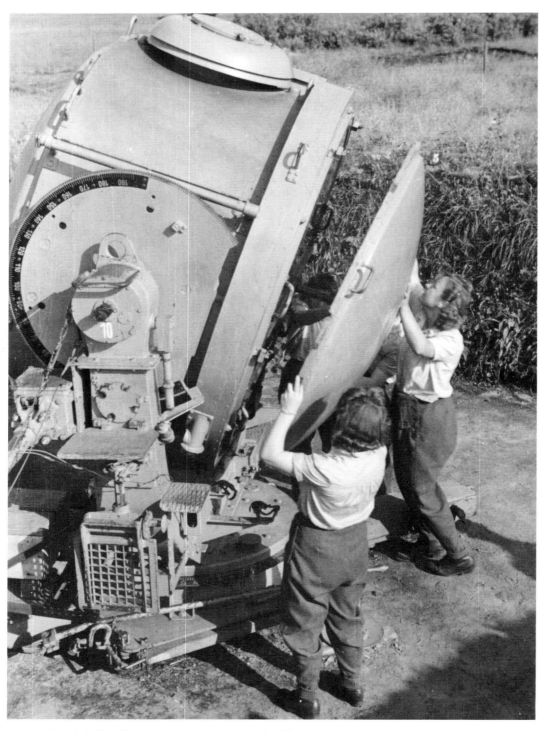

Along with male Luftwaffe helpers, women also served as Flak-weapon helpers on listening devices and searchlights. Here the heavy cover of a 150 cm searchlight is being removed by them. (BA)

A Flak Oberleutnant and women helpers operate a 200 cm searchlight. (BA)

Women Flak-weapon helpers are being trained on the Flak Aiming Device 40 A. By using this device, equipped with two binocular scopes, a target could be engaged optically and the targeting values transmitted to the searchlights by Transmission Device 37 via indicators. (BA)

Alarm! Women Flak helpers hurry to their RRH listening device. (BA)

The crew is in place at the H9 listening device and is putting on headsets. H7 is still standing at the calculator. The traverse listener (H8) sits at the left side of the device and is partly obscured by it. (BA)

Croatian volunteers, recognizable by the emblems on their left sleeves, are inspected by German officers at the end of their training as Flak soldiers. (BA)

Croatian volunteers operating a fixed 20 mm Flak quad. (BA)

Below: Only three crewmen of this 88 mm Flak gun wear the German emblem on their caps. The others are apparently all volunteers. (BA)

How the other side regarded the German Flak guns then is expressed clearly in reports of the 8th and 9th U.S. Air Fleets:

"In the European theater of war, the German Flak has always been a great source of danger. In 1943, 1/3 of the total losses of bombers and 2/3 of the damaged aircraft were attributable to them."

The damage done to the bombers by the German Flak weapons reached its pinnacle in April 1944. Flak positions that were not literally overrun continued to offer stubborn resistance to all bomb attacks. In June, July and August 1944, the Flak guns were responsible for some 2/3 of the 700 total losses of bombers and up to 98% of the approximately 1300 that returned with damage (12,687 were hit by Flak fire and only 182 by fighter-plane weapons).

In the last months before the end of September 1944, between 3,360 and 4,453 Allied bombers per month returned with Flak damage.

In tactical service, the question was constantly asked: Where are the cursed German Flak positions located?

In a concluding report, General Arnold stated: "We never conquered the German Flak artillery; it was never 'kaputt' before it surrendered with the rest of the Wehrmacht on May 7, 1945."

These excerpts show some Allied views of the German Flak. May these citations strengthen the awareness of the Flak artillerymen of the last war, their brave helpers, the soldiers of the Luftwaffe intelligence units, the homeland Flak soldiers, the RAD Flak men and women, the male and female Luftwaffe and Flak-weapon helpers, and of many others, that they belonged to a troop that did their soldierly duty with bravery and honor.

An 88 mm Flak gun crosses the upper Rhine on a ferry in 1940.

An NCO of an 88 mm Flak battery uses searchlight aiming binoculars to observe the sky near Sprendlingen.

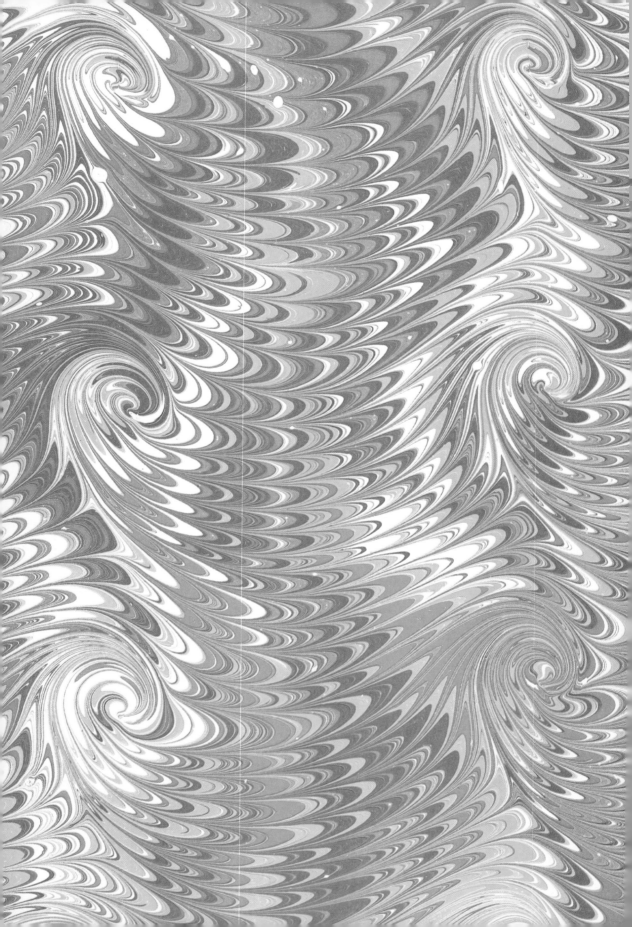